THE VICTORIANS

Book of Days

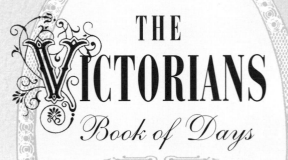

THE VICTORIANS
Book of Days

A NOSTALGIC GLIMPSE OF A BYGONE ERA

Joanne Jessop

COOMBE BOOKS

The Victorian Era

Queen Victoria reigned from 1837 to 1901, longer than any previous British monarch. During her reign, Britain was the most prosperous industrial nation in the world, with an ever-expanding overseas empire. It was a time of technological progress, expansion, optimism and change. But in the midst of these rapidly changing times Queen Victoria provided a sense of stability and respectability. She ruled with dignity, setting the moral standard for the nation and giving her name to the age in which she lived.

The Victorians loved their queen and were proudly nationalistic. Admiration for Queen and country was part of the social fabric and a theme that every child learned at school.

Beautiful England – on her island throne –
Grandly she rules, with half the world her own.
From her vast empire the sun ne'er departs:
She reigns a Queen – Victoria, Queen of Hearts.

This year book looks back in fondness on some of the pastimes, delights and foibles of Victorian society. It provides images of the times and records of the thoughts, reflections and reactions of those who lived through this interesting and memorable period of history.

The rich man in his castle,
The poor man at his gate,
God made them, high and lowly,
And ordered their estate.

CECIL FRANCES ALEXANDER
(1818–1895)
HYMN (1848)

JANUARY

ICTORIAN SOCIETY was very class conscious. And the commonly held belief, as expressed in the famous hymn written in 1848 by Mrs C. F. Alexander, was that nothing should be done to interfere with the divinely ordained pattern of social life. There was little movement between the rigid class boundaries; people knew their place in society and with few exceptions were content to stay there.

Class Distinctions

AT THE TOP of the social hierarchy was the Queen and her court, and it was from here that values, morals and behaviour trickled down to the rest of society. The higher classes saw it as their duty to set an example for those below them.

Each class of society has its own requirements; but it may be said that every class teaches the one immediately below it; and if the highest class be ignorant, uneducated, loving display, luxurious, and idle, the same spirit will prevail in humbler life.

GIRLS' HOME COMPANION (1895)

It is impossible, in our condition of society, not to be sometimes a snob.

WILLIAM MAKEPEACE THACKERAY
(1811–1863)
BOOK OF SNOBS

1

2

3

4

5

6

7

NOTES

JANUARY

Society and the Season

THE RICH who made up 'Society' divided their time between their country homes and London. The 'London Season', between May and August, was a constant round of social engagements and entertainment. And the pinnacle of success for any daughter of Society was a presentation at Court.

It is an epoch in a woman's life not easily forgotten. To a young girl it signifies transition from girlhood to womanhood; from the obscurity of the schoolroom to the brilliancy of society life, in which at-homes, dinners, balls, garden parties, operas and theatres follow each other in a continuous whirl. The smile of the Queen had transformed the little homely grub into a gay butterfly.

THE HARMSWORTH MAGAZINE (1900)

The London season officially extends from Royal Academy opening in May until 12th August, when the centre of society's interests shift to the grouse moors.

MRS. BEETON (1836–1865)
BOOK OF HOUSEHOLD MANAGEMENT

JANUARY

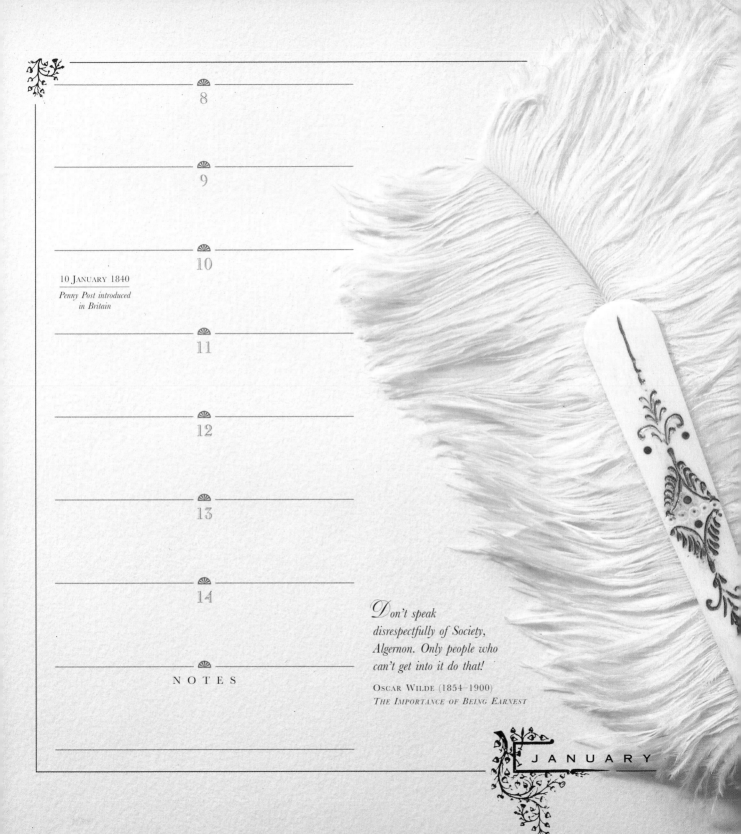

8

9

10

10 JANUARY 1840

*Penny Post introduced
in Britain*

11

12

13

14

NOTES

*Don't speak
disrespectfully of Society,
Algernon. Only people who
can't get into it do that!*

OSCAR WILDE (1854–1900)
THE IMPORTANCE OF BEING EARNEST

JANUARY

Balls and Dances

BALL AND DANCES were the means by which a young girl was introduced into Society. But no young girl attended without a chaperon, usually her mother or some other married woman. She stayed close to her chaperon until asked to dance and was quickly returned to the chaperon's protection after each turn on the dance floor. To dance more than three times with the same partner was considered forward and would inevitably lead to rumours of the couple's engagement.

The delight of the average hostess's heart is the well-bred man, unspoiled by conceit, who can always be depended upon to do his duty. He arrives in good time, fills his card before very long, and can be asked to dance with a plain, neglected wallflower or two without resenting it. He takes his partner duly to the refreshment-room after each dance, if she wishes to go, and provides her with whatever she wishes. Before leaving her, he sees her safe at her chaperone's side.

MRS HUMPHRY
MANNERS FOR MEN (1897)

JANUARY

15

16

17

18

19

20

21

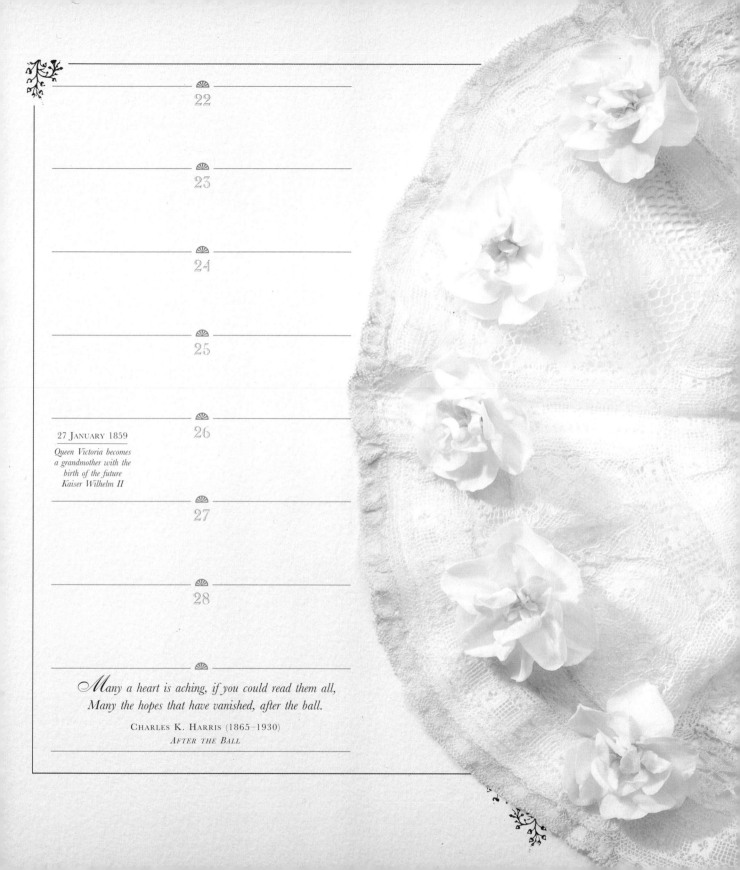

22

23

24

25

27 January 1859

*Queen Victoria becomes
a grandmother with the
birth of the future
Kaiser Wilhelm II*

26

27

28

*Many a heart is aching, if you could read them all,
Many the hopes that have vanished, after the ball.*

CHARLES K. HARRIS (1865–1930)
After the Ball

29

30

31

NOTES

Social Etiquette

THE STRICT RULES OF ETIQUETTE for almost every aspect of Victorian life were obligingly explained in numerous books of manners. These guides to good manners were designed to help the growing numbers of middle-class women through the social pitfalls of attending their first ball or giving their first dinner party. By far the most famous guide book was Mrs Beeton's *Book of Household Management*, which included tips on good manners and etiquette as well as useful household information such as how to prepare and present a dinner for forty. Good manners and etiquette were based on the principle of sparing the other person's feelings, yet in a society with so many social rigours it was sometimes necessary to let people know when their behaviour was not acceptable – but always with delicacy and tact.

Tact is both innate and acquired . . . and though a delicate sense of what is due to others is of the very essence of tact, it is never quite perfect without a knowledge of the gentle art of snubbing. This is an accomplishment some women never acquire . . . Where they should simply ignore, they administer a cut direct . . . The 'retort courteous' loses none of its point for being courteous.

MRS HUMPHRY
MANNERS FOR WOMEN (1897)

Good breeding consists of concealing how much we think of ourselves and how little we think of the other person.

MARK TWAIN (1835–1910)
UNPUBLISHED DIARIES

The truth is that society demands a never-ending series of self-denying actions from those who belong to it, and the more cheerfully these are performed, the more perfect the manners.

MRS HUMPHRY
MANNERS FOR MEN (1897)

*She will tend him, nurse
him, mend him,
Air his linen dry his tears;
Bless the thoughtful fates that
send him
Such a wife to soothe his years!*

W. S. GILBERT (1836–1911)
THE SORCERER

*Teacher, tender comrade, wife,
A fellow-farer true through life,
Heart-whole and soul-free,
The august Father gave to me.*

ROBERT LOUIS STEVENSON
(1850–1894)
MY WIFE

FEBRUARY

N VICTORIAN SOCIETY it was the wife's role to preside over the home and provide a haven of tranquillity and stability for her husband. She was 'The Angel of the House' – a phrase that was used as the title of Coventry Patmore's popular poem about married love.

Love and Marriage

Whene'er I come where ladies are,
　　How sad soever I was before,
Though like a ship frost-bound and far
　　Withheld in ice from the ocean's roar,
Third-winter'd in that dreadful dock,
　　With stiffen'd cordage, sail decay'd,
And crew that care for calm and shock
　　Alike, too dull to be dismay'd,
Yet, if I come where ladies are,
　　How sad soever I was before,
Then is my sadness banish'd far,
　　And I am like that ship no more;
Or like that ship if the ice-field splits,
　　Burst by the sudden polar Spring,
And all thank God with their warming wits,
　　And kiss each other and dance and sing,
And hoist fresh sails, that make the breeze
　　Blow them along the liquid sea,
Out of the North, where life did freeze,
　　Into the haven where they would be.

COVENTRY PATMORE (1823–1896)
An Angel in the House

1

2

3

4

5

6

7

NOTES

FEBRUARY

_____ 8

_____ 9

_____ 10

10 FEBRUARY 1840

*Queen Victoria marries
Prince Albert*

_____ 11

_____ 12

_____ 13

_____ 14

_____

NOTES

Love and Marriage

*Happiness untold awaits them
When the parson consecrates them.*

W. S. GILBERT (1836–1911)
RUDDIGORE

VICTORIA AND ALBERT set the standards for the perfect marriage. They were young, good-looking and in love. The Victorians put great emphasis on love and romance and it was the favourite subject of some of the greatest poets of the day.

*She gave me eyes, she gave me ears;
And humble cares, and delicate fears;
A heart, the fountain of sweet tears;
And love, and thought, and joy.*

WILLIAM WORDSWORTH (1770–1850)
THE SPARROW'S NEST (REFERRING TO HIS WIFE)

FEBRUARY

A courage to endure and obey;
A hate of gossip parlance, and of sway,
Crown'd Isabel, thro' all her placid life,
The queen of marriage, a most perfect wife.

ALFRED, LORD TENNYSON (1809–1892)
ISABEL

How do I love thee? Let me count the ways
  I love thee to the depth and breadth and height
My soul can reach, when feeling out of sight
  For the ends of Being and ideal Grace.
I love thee to the level of everyday's
  Most quiet need, by sun and candlelight.
I love thee freely, as men strive for Right;
  I love thee purely, as they turn from Praise.
I love thee with the passion put to use
  In my old griefs, and with my childhood's faith.
I love thee with a love I seemed to lose
  With my lost saints, – I love thee with the breath,
Smile, tears, of all my life! – and, if God choose,
  I shall but love thee better after death.

ELIZABETH BARRETT BROWNING (1806–1861)
SONNETS FROM THE PORTUGUESE

Marriage is of so much use to a woman, opens
out to her so much more of life, and puts her in the way of so
much more freedom and usefulness, whether she marry well or ill,
she can hardly miss some benefit.

ROBERT LOUIS STEVENSON (1850–1894)
VIRGINIBUS PUERISQUE

F E B R U A R Y

Introductions and Social Calls

INTRODUCTIONS and social calls were an important feature of Victorian social life. But even a seeming simple thing like an introduction was not without its pitfalls; one Victorian manual on manner warns:

An introduction is a social endorsement, and you become, to a certain extent, responsible for the person you introduce. If he disgraces himself in any way you share, in a greater or lesser degree, in his disgrace.

ANONYMOUS
HOW TO BEHAVE – A POCKET MANUAL OF ETIQUETTE

Mrs Charles Freeman
38 The Avenue
Brighton

dy Harrison
at home
20th February
12 FLORENCE GARDENS, WASHINGTON

When acquaintances chanced upon each other in the street, the rules of etiquette again governed their behaviour. Here is Mrs Humphry's advice to the well-bred gentleman:

In meeting acquaintances a nod is sufficient for a male friend, unless his age or position is such as to render it advisable to raise the hat. Should a lady be with the acquaintance any man meeting them must raise his hat. So must the individual walking with the lady. The etiquette of bowing is a simple one. Male acquaintances always wait for acknowledgement on the part of the female, as well as from those of men who are their superiors in age or position.

MRS HUMPHRY
MANNERS FOR MEN (1897)

FEBRUARY

_____ 15

_____ 16

_____ 17

_____ 18

_____ 19

20 FEBRUARY 1896

Lumière brothers of France give a display of films in London

_____ 20

_____ 21

NOTES

ONCE A SOCIAL ACQUAINTANCE was established, the next step was the social call. Some women set fixed days for being 'at home' for social callers. The call was expected to be short, not more than fifteen minutes, and on the way out visiting cards were left on the hall table, where they stayed for other visitors to see.

There is very strict etiquette in this matter of cards and calls . . . It is usual on paying a first visit merely to leave cards without inquiring if the mistress of the house is at home. Thus Mrs. A. leaves her own card and two of her husband's cards upon Mrs. B. Within a week, if possible, certainly within ten days Mrs. B. should return the visit and leave cards upon Mrs. A. Should Mrs. A., however, have 'called' upon Mrs. B. and the latter returned it by merely leaving cards this would be a sign that the latter did not desire the acquaintance to ripen into friendship.

THE LADY, A MAGAZINE FOR GENTLEWOMEN (9 FEBRUARY 1893)

Terence
e ~ Jeavons

The Manor
Waterbridge, Suffolk

FEBRUARY

Victorian Sundays

A VICTORIAN SUNDAY was often the dullest day of the week. After morning church there were few 'proper' Sunday activities to be enjoyed. Those who wished to go out were limited in what they could do since almost everything was closed for the day. Even the art galleries did not have Sunday openings until 1896. Children were expected to give up their toys and games for the day and engage in some uplifting reading.

There was the dreary Sunday of his childhood, when he sat with his hands before him, scared out of his senses by a horrible tract which commenced business with the poor child by asking him in the title, why he was going to Perdition? – a piece of curiosity that he really in a frock and drawers was not in a condition to satisfy . . . There was the sleepy Sunday of his boyhood, when, like a military deserter, he was marched to chapel by a picquet of teachers three times a day, morally handcuffed to another boy . . . There was the interminable Sunday of his nonage; when his mother, stern of face and unrelenting of heart, would sit all day behind a Bible – bound, like her own construction of it, in the hardest, barest, and straitest boards . . .

CHARLES DICKENS (1812–1870)
LITTLE DORRIT

It was Sunday afternoon, wet and cheerless: and a duller spectacle this earth of ours has not to show than a rainy Sunday in London.

THOMAS DE QUINCEY (1785–1859)

FEBRUARY

_____ ⁂ 22 _____

_____ ⁂ 23 _____

_____ ⁂ 24 _____

_____ ⁂ 25 _____

_____ ⁂ 26 _____

_____ ⁂ 27 _____

_____ ⁂ 28 _____

_____ ⁂ _____
NOTES

*On Sundays, all our toys and games were put away.
Even our sewing and embroidery were forbidden. All afternoon
my sister and I, dressed in our best frocks, stiff with starch,
ribbons and bows, would sit in the parlour with the
grown-ups reading solemn religious tracts and waiting for
the long interminable Sunday to be over.*

DOROTHY FRASER (1839–1925)
PERSONAL REMINISCENCES

FEBRUARY

MARCH

HILDREN were expected to learn by rote, verses with strong moral themes. Lewis Carroll's verse below parodies the famous poem *Against Idleness and Mischief* opposite, which many Victorian children knew by heart.

How doth the little crocodile
  Improve his shining tail,
And pour the waters of the Nile
  On every golden scale!

How cheerfully he seems to grin,
  How neatly spreads his claws,
And welcomes little fishes in
  With gently smiling jaws.

LEWIS CARROLL (1832–1898) *HOW DOTH THE LITTLE CROCODILE*

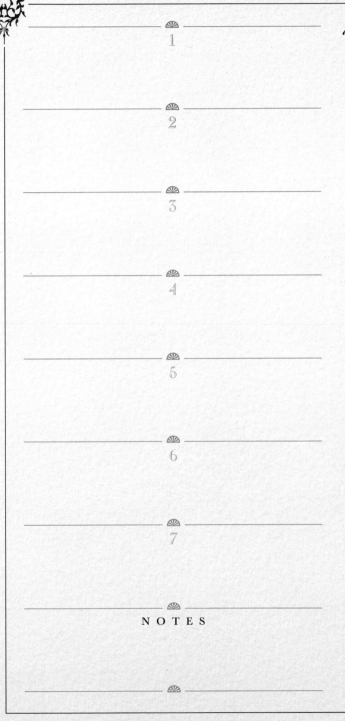

1

2

3

4

5

6

7

NOTES

'Improving' Verses
for Children

How doth the little busy bee
    Improve each shining hour,
And gather honey all the day
    From every opening flower!

How skilfully she builds her cell!
    How neat she spreads the wax!
And labours hard to store it well
    With the sweet food she makes.

In works of labour or of skill,
    I would be busy too;
For Satan finds some mischief still
    For idle hands to do.

In books, or work, or healthful play,
    Let my first years be passed,
That I may give for every day
    Some good account at last.

DR ISAAC WATTS (1674–1748)
AGAINST IDLENESS AND MISCHIEF

The Countryside

AS MORE AND MORE Victorians moved into the industrial towns and cities, they discovered a great interest in 'Nature' and the countryside, which was reflected in the poems and writings of the time.

As the art of life is learned, it will be found at last that all lovely things are also necessary – the wild flowers by the wayside as well as the tended corn; and the weird birds and creatures of the forest as well as the tended cattle; because man doth not live by bread only, but also by the dearest manna, by every wondrous word and unknowable work of God.

JOHN RUSKIN (1819–1900)

Before green apples blush,
Before green nuts embrown,
Why, one day in the country
Is worth a month in town.

CHRISTINA ROSSETTI (1830–1894)
SUMMER

Earth's crammed with heaven,
And every common bush afire with God.

ELIZABETH BARRETT BROWNING
(1806–1861)
AURORA LEIGH

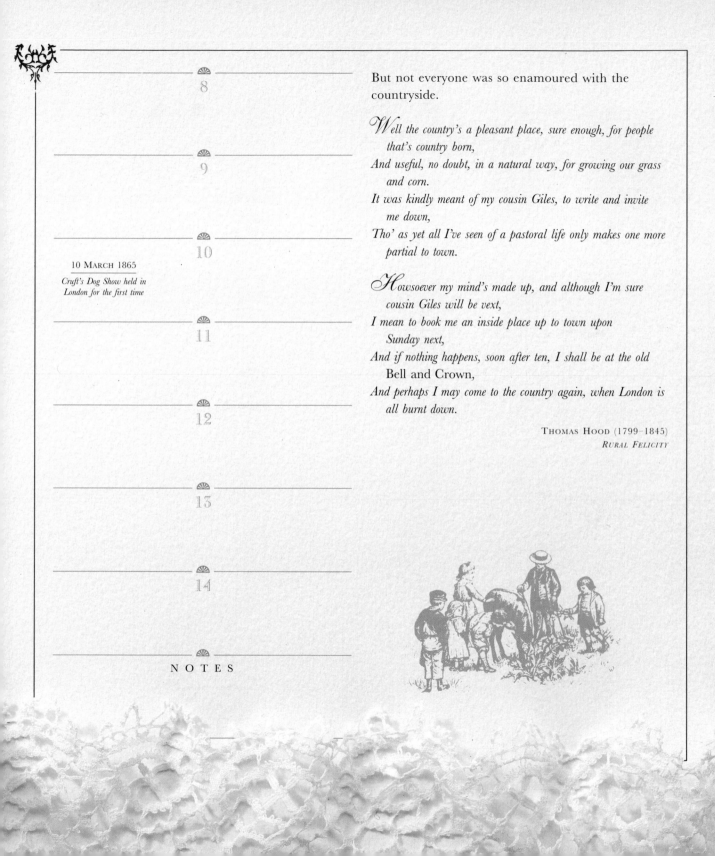

8

9

10

10 MARCH 1865

*Cruft's Dog Show held in
London for the first time*

11

12

13

14

NOTES

But not everyone was so enamoured with the
countryside.

*Well the country's a pleasant place, sure enough, for people
that's country born,*
*And useful, no doubt, in a natural way, for growing our grass
and corn.*
*It was kindly meant of my cousin Giles, to write and invite
me down,*
*Tho' as yet all I've seen of a pastoral life only makes one more
partial to town.*

*Howsoever my mind's made up, and although I'm sure
cousin Giles will be vext,*
*I mean to book me an inside place up to town upon
Sunday next,*
*And if nothing happens, soon after ten, I shall be at the old
Bell and Crown,*
*And perhaps I may come to the country again, when London is
all burnt down.*

THOMAS HOOD (1799–1845)
RURAL FELICITY

Country Walks

DURING THE VICTORIAN ERA, country walking became a favourite pastime for many town dwellers. On Sundays and bank holidays, clerks and factory workers, on their own or with families in tow, would set out on their bicycles or by train for a day in the countryside. Walking through the fields and meadows and along country lanes they came to appreciate the peace and beauty of the rural scenery around them.

I never wholly feel that summer is high,
However green the trees, or loud the birds,
However movelessly eye-winking herds
Stand in field ponds, or under large trees lie,
Till I do climb all cultured pastures by,
That hedged by hedgerows studiously fretted trim,
Smile like a lady's face with lace laced prim,
And on some moor or hill that seeks the sky
Lonely and nakedly, – utterly lie down,
And feel the sunshine throbbing on body and limb,
My drowsy brain in pleasant drunkenness swim,
Each rising thought sink back and dreamily drown,
Smiles creep o'er my face, and smother my lips, and cloy,
Each muscle sink to itself, and separately enjoy.

EBENEZER JONES (1820–1860)
HIGH SUMMER

15

16

17

18

19

20

21

NOTES

22

23

24

25

26

27

28

NOTES

25 MARCH 1843

Opening of the Thames Tunnel, completed by Isambard Brunel

*G*od made the country,
and man made the town.

WILLIAM COWPER (1731–1800)
TABLETALK

*D*ainty little maiden,
whither would you wander?
Whither from this pretty house,
this city-house of ours?
'Far and far away,' said the
dainty little maiden,
'All among the meadows, the
clover and the clematis,
Daisies and kingcups and
honeysuckle-flowers.'

ALFRED, LORD TENNYSON
(1809–1892)
THE CITY CHILD

MARCH

Mountain Climbing

MOUNTAIN CLIMBING for pleasure came into vogue during the early years of the nineteenth century. By Victorian times, many adventurous men, and sometimes women, were travelling to Europe to climb the Swiss Alps. Before long, all the highest mountains of Europe had been climbed.

Oh! when I have hung
Above the raven's nest, by knots of grass
And half-inch fissures in the slippery rock
But ill sustained, and almost (so it seemed)
Suspended by the blast that blew amain,
Shouldering the naked crag, oh, at that time
While on the perilous ridge I hung alone,
With what strange utterance did the loud dry wind
Blow through my ear! the sky seemed not a sky
Of earth — and with what motion moved the clouds!

WILLIAM WORDSWORTH (1770–1850)
THE PRELUDE

Double the labour of my task
But give, oh! give me what I ask,
The sunlight and the mountain air.

ELIZA COOK (1818–1889)

Mountains are the beginning and the end of all natural scenery.

JOHN RUSKIN (1819–1900)
MODERN PAINTERS

_____
          29

_____
          30

_____
          31

_____
        N O T E S

_____

_____

_____

_____

_____

_____

Come away with me, Tom,
  Term and talk are done;
My poor lads are reaping,
  Busy every one.
Curates mind the parish,
  Sweepers mind the court;
We'll away to Snowdon
  For our ten days' sport . . .
Up a thousand feet, Tom,
  Round the lion's head,
Find soft stones to leeward
  And make up our bed.
Eat our bread and bacon,
  Smoke the pipe of peace,
And, ere we be drowsy,
  Give our boots a grease.

CHARLES KINGSLEY (1819–1875)
THE INVITATION

APRIL

THE PENNY-FARTHING bicycle, with its giant front wheel and small back wheel, was a Victorian invention. But it was not designed for the faint-hearted; it required considerable skill to ride and could be hazardous. When the 'safety' bicycle, with chain drive and air-filled tyres, was introduced in the 1880s more people took to the roads. It soon became the height of fashion to ride a bicycle.

2

3

4

5

6

7

NOTES

Bicycles

The spring of '96 saw us in Torquay . . . everybody was learning to ride things called bicycles. In Torquay there was a circular cinder-track where, at stated hours, men and women rode solemnly round. Tailors supplied special costumes for this sport.

RUDYARD KIPLING (1865–1936)

With lifted feet, hands still,
 I am poised, and down the hill
Dart, with heedful mind;
 The air goes by in a wind.

Swifter and yet more swift,
 Till the heart with a mighty lift
Makes the lungs laugh, the throat cry: –
 'O bird, see; see, bird, I fly.'

HENRY CHARLES BEECHING (1859–1919)
GOING DOWN HILL ON A BICYCLE

The Bloomer Girls

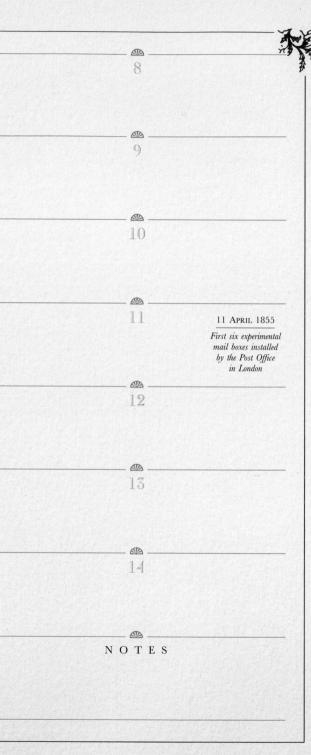

WOMEN CYCLISTS often found themselves being spilt on to the road when their long skirts became tangled up into gears and spokes. An American woman, Mrs Amelia Bloomer, designed a more practical and safer cycling costume – long, full trousers that tied at the ankle. This garment, nicknamed 'bloomers', scandalized many respectable Victorians, and poor Mrs Bloomer was even accused of trying to undermine the very foundation of the family. She and her 'bloomer girls' suffered much ridicule and were the butt of many rude jokes and songs, like this popular music hall number:

I'LL BE A BLOOMER

Listen, females all
    No matter what your trade is,
Old Nick is in the girls,
    The Devil's in the ladies!
Married men may weep,
    And tumble in the ditches,
Since women are resolved
    To wear the shirts and breeches.

Ladies do declare
    A change should have been sooner,
The women one and all,
    Are going to join the Bloomers.
Prince Albert and the Queen
    Had such a jolly row, sirs;
She threw off her stays and put
    On waistcoat, coat and trousers.

APRIL

8

9

10

11

11 APRIL 1855

First six experimental mail boxes installed by the Post Office in London

12

13

14

NOTES

15

16

17

18

18 April 1873
—
David Livingstone
buried at Westminster
Abbey

19

20

21

NOTES

APRIL

Safely a... aven.

Railways

RAILWAYS were a product of the nineteenth century and the industrial revolution. In 1825, the Stockton to Darlington line became the first railway to carry passengers. Within a decade, a network of railway lines to criss-cross Victorian England had been mapped out and construction was under way.

Faster than the fairies, faster than witches,
   Bridges and houses, hedges and ditches;
And charging along like troops in a battle,
   All through the meadows the houses and cattle;
And all of the sights of the hill and the plain
   Fly as thick as driving rain;
And ever again, in the wink of an eye,
   Painted stations whistle by.

Here is a child who clambers and scrambles,
   All by himself and gathering brambles;
Here is a tramp who stands and gazes;
   And here is the green for stringing the daisies!
Here is a cart run away in the road
   Lumping along with man and load;
And here is a mill, there is a river;
   Each a glimpse and gone for ever!

ROBERT LOUIS STEVENSON (1850–1894)
FROM A RAILWAY CARRIAGE

APRIL

22

23

24

25

26

27

28

NOTES

*At nine in the morning
there passed a church,
    At ten there passed me by the sea,
At twelve a town of smoke and smirch,
    At two a forest of oak and birch,
        And then, on the platform, she:*

*A radiant stranger who saw not me,
    I said 'Get out to her do I dare?'
But I kept my seat in my search for a plea,
    And the wheels moved on. O could it but be
        That I had alighted there!*

THOMAS HARDY (1840–1928)
FAINTHEART IN A RAILWAY TRAIN

APRIL

Railways

I see no reason to suppose that these machines will ever force themselves into general use.

THE DUKE OF WELLINGTON (1769–1852)

DESPITE THIS PROPHESY, the railways soon became an indispensable part of Victorian life, offering unprecedented speed and comfort and new scope for travel and holidays. With the railways came day trips to the countryside or to the seaside, although Sunday travel was frowned upon by some respectable Victorians.

Going by railroad I do not consider travelling at all; it is merely being 'sent' to a place, and very little different from becoming a parcel.

JOHN RUSKIN (1819–1900)
MODERN PAINTERS

APRIL

NOTES

'*I* fear there is a great deal of Sabbath travelling here,' said he [Mr Slope]. 'On looking at the "Bradshaw", I see that there are three trains in and three trains out every Sabbath. Could nothing be done to induce the company to withdraw them? Don't you think, Dr Grantly, that a little energy might diminish the evil?'

'Not being a director, I really can't say. But if you withdraw the passengers, the company, I dare say, will withdraw the trains,' said the doctor. 'It's merely a question of dividends.'

ANTHONY TROLLOPE (1815–1882)
BARCHESTER TOWERS

MAY

N 1 MAY 1851, Queen Victoria opened the Great Exhibition of the Works of Industry of all Nations, a showcase of technology, science and art, which had been inspired and supported by Prince Albert. This was the first international exhibition of its kind and drew hundreds of thousands of visitors from all over the world.

1

2

3

4

5

6

7

N O T E S

The Great Exhibition

THE GREAT EXHIBITION HALL was a magnificent glass building, 1,848 feet long, 408 feet wide and 66 feet high, that enclosed some of the finest elm trees growing in Hyde Park. This masterpiece of design and engineering was dubbed 'The Crystal Palace' by the satirical magazine *Punch*.

*This is one of the greatest
and most glorious days of
our lives, with which to my
pride and joy the name of
my dearly beloved Albert is
forever associated! It is a day
which makes my heart swell
with thankfulness.*

QUEEN VICTORIA'S DIARY
(1 MAY 1851)

*Fairy Giant choicest birth
Of the Beautiful Sublime,
Seeming like the Toy of earth
Given to the dotard Time, –
Glacier-diamond, Alp of glass,
Sinbad's cave, Aladdin's hall, –
Must it then be crush'd, alas;
Must the Crystal Palace fall?*

ANONYMOUS
THE GREAT EXHIBITION

MAY

8

9

10

11

12

13

14

NOTES

MAY

Parks

THE VICTORIAN AGE saw a great increase in the number of public parks, walks and open spaces in the cities and towns. These new city parks usually had a bandstand surrounded by wooden chairs, where in fine weather bands could entertain park users. But parks were seen as more than just a place of entertainment and enjoyment. There were the obvious health benefits of exercise in the open air, and more subtle social benefits as well. It was hoped that these recreational facilities would draw the working man away from the pub and put him and his family in contact with the superior examples of the higher classes. Here is one of the arguments extolling the social virtues of public parks put before a standing committee by a Member of Parliament:

A man walking out with his family among his neighbours of different ranks, will naturally be desirous to be properly clothed, and that his wife should be also; but this desire duly directed and controlled, is found by experience to be of the most powerful effect in promoting Civilisation and exciting industry.

STANDING COMMITTEE ON PUBLIC WALKS (1833)

Here in this sequester'd close
Bloom the hyacinth and rose,
Here beside the modest stock
Flaunts the flaring hollyhock . . .

HENRY AUSTIN DOBSON (1840–1921)
A GARDEN SONG

MAY

Gardens

THE IMPROVED AMENITIES and comforts of the new middle-class homes included gardens, and gardening became a great Victorian pastime. Thousands of new plants became available to the gardener, from exotic shrubs to geometrically-planted geraniums.

IN THE ROSE GARDEN
THOMAS JAMES LLOYD (1849–1910)

The kiss of the sun for pardon
The song of the birds for mirth,
One is nearer God's heart in a garden
Than anywhere else on earth.

DOROTHY FRANCES GURNEY (1858–1932)
THE LORD GOD PLANTED A GARDEN

No man feels more of a man in the world if he have but a bit of ground that he can call his own. However small it is on the surface, it is four thousand miles deep; and that is a very handsome property.

CHARLES DUDLEY WARNER (1829–1900)

MAY

15

16

17

17 MAY 1861
The beginning of Thomas Cook's first continental holiday tour – six days in Paris

18

19

20

20 MAY 1895
First film ever shown to a paying audience, displayed in New York city

21

NOTES

22

23

24

24 May 1819

Victoria born at Kensington Palace, London

25

26

27

28

NOTES

*F*loriculture
and horticulture
while being health
giving is also a pure
and harmless recreation,
which may be engaged in
by individuals of either sex
and of all stations of life, the
peasant as well as the peer, the
overtoiled man of business and the
industrious artisan, on every
imaginable scale from a single flower
pot to the princely conservatory.

BANBURY GUARDIAN (1866)

MAY

Summer Sports

CROQUET, imported from Ireland in the 1850s, became popular with the city-dwelling middle classes because all it needed was a small lawn and a croquet set. Lawn tennis, invented in 1874, was taken up by the middle classes for the same reason.

In 1877, the first Wimbledon tennis Championships included both men and women. Archery was considered a graceful sport for ladies, and the Women's Archery association was established in 1864.

Every sporting activity required fashionable costumes, which were not always conducive to carefree enjoyment, especially for women. The following passage shows some of the hazards of rowing with 'prettily dressed' women:

Girls don't look half bad in a boat, if prettily dressed. Nothing is more fetching to my way of thinking than a tasteful boating costume . . . [The girls] were both beautifully got up — all lace and silky stuff, and flowers, and ribbons, and dainty shoes, and light gloves . . . and try as I would, I could not help the occasional flicker of water from going over these dresses. The girls did not complain, but they huddled up close together, and set their lips firm, and every time a drop touched them, they visibly shrank and shuddered. It was a noble sight to see them suffering in silence, but it unnerved me altogether.

JEROME K. JEROME (1859–1927)
THREE MEN IN A BOAT

MAY

_____

⚜
29

_____

⚜
30

_____

⚜
31

_____

⚜
NOTES

_____

⚜

_____

⚜

_____

⚜

_____

⚜

_____

*At Croquet, Croquet,
a proper game to play,
At Croquet, Croquet, I could
play all day,
There's nothing can surpass,
the sport upon the grass
In that Awfully Jolly game
call'd Croquet.*

POPULAR SONG

MAY

JUNE

 UEEN VICTORIA AND HER FAMILY were very
fond of picnics, and in this, as in so many
other aspects of Victorian life, the royal family
set the standard. A Victorian picnic tended to
be an elaborate affair that required a great
deal of work and planning.

1

2

3

4

5

6

7

NOTES

Picnics

The table rises like magic from under the lid of the picnic hamper. The butter emerges from the cool retreat, glass-lined, within its own particular box. The salt, without whose savour many a dead and gone picnic had to be content, is provided in sufficiency in receptacles with tightly-fitting lids. The whole paraphernalia for tea in the woods or on the river is supplied in the same way . . . and if something of the improvisation and extemporaneous is missing from the picnic today, they are qualities appreciated only by the very young.

MRS HUMPHRY
MANNERS FOR WOMEN (1897)

*There, on a slope of orchard, Francis laid
A damask napkin wrought with horse and hound,
Brought out a dusky loaf that smelt of home,
And, half-cut-down, a pasty costly-made,
Where quail and pigeon, lark and leveret lay,
Like fossils of the rock, with golden yolks
Imbedded and injellied; last, with these,
A flask of cider from his father's vats,
Prime, which I knew; and so we sat and eat
And talk'd old matters over; who was dead,
Who married, who was like to be, and how
The races went, and who would rent
the hall . . .*

ALFRED, LORD TENNYSON (1809–1892)
AUDLEY COURT

JUNE

Boating

THE HENLEY ROYAL REGATTA was inaugurated in 1839 at Henley-on-Thames in England in response to a growing interest in boat races like the one between Oxford and Cambridge, which first took place at Henley in 1829. The Henley Regatta soon became part of the summer social calendar.

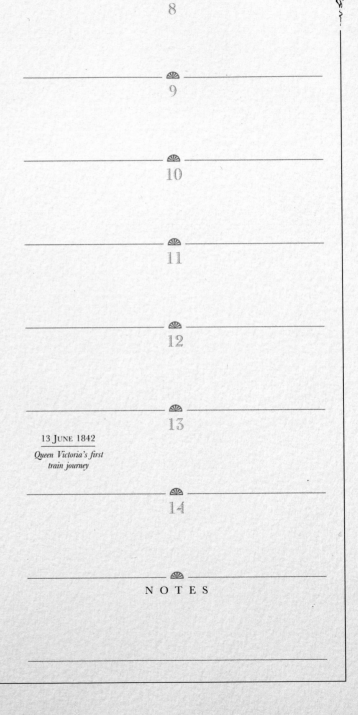

8

9

10

11

12

13

13 June 1842
Queen Victoria's first
train journey

14

NOTES

BOATING gained even more enthusiasts after the publication in 1889 of Jerome K. Jerome's book *Three Men in a Boat*. However, on reading this passage, it is a wonder it didn't have the opposite effect:

Sailing is a thing that wants knowledge and practice too – though as a boy, I did not think so . . . I knew a boy who thought likewise, and so, one windy day, we thought we would try the sport . . .

That the boat did not upset I simply state as a fact. Why it did not upset I am unable to offer any reason. I have often thought about the matter since, but I have never succeeded in arriving at any satisfactory explanation of the phenomenon.

Possibly the result may have been brought about by the natural obstinacy of all things in the world. The boat may possibly have come to the conclusion, judging from a cursory view of our behaviour, that we had come out for a morning's suicide, and had therefore determined to disappoint us. That is the only suggestion I can offer.

By clinging like grim death to the gunwale, we just managed to keep inside the boat, but it was exhausting work . . . The boat travelled up-stream for about a mile at a pace I have never sailed at since, and don't want to again. Then, at a bend, she heeled over till half her sail was under water. Then she righted herself by a miracle and flew for a long low bank of soft mud.

JEROME K. JEROME (1859–1927)
THREE MEN IN A BOAT

JUNE

*Are you going to
Scarborough fair?
Parsley, sage, rosemary
and thyme.
Remember me to one
who lives there.
She once was a true
love of mine.*

TRADITIONAL SONG

*As I was going to Derby,
All on a market day,
I met the finest ram, sir,
That ever was fed upon hay.*

ANONYMOUS

*To market, to market, to buy a fat pig;
Home again, home again, jiggety jig.
To market, to market, to buy a fine hog;
Home again, home again, joggety jog.*

NURSERY RHYME

JUNE

15

16

17

18

19

20

20 JUNE 1837
*Victoria becomes Queen
of Britain*

21

NOTES

Fairs

THE ANNUAL FAIR was the highlight of rural life, probably the greatest event on the local calendar. Almost every village had their own fair or summer fête, but the larger fairs were generally held in a market town. The importance of fairs as great trading events declined during the Victorian era, but nevertheless they did attract dealers from all over the country who came to buy and sell livestock, corn and cloth. But there were other, more exciting, visitors to the fair as well – gypsies, jugglers, conjurers, quacks, Punch and Judy men, dancing bears, performing monkeys and many more entertainers.

A fair could last a week and include a vast array of entertainment and wonder. Here is a description of the Nottingham Goose Fair of 1850:

Exhibition of all kinds of things, Saloons of Art, Fat Pigs, a Mammoth Ox and other monstrosities too tedious to mention. There are panoramas, illuminated models, conjuring shows and lastly, the funeral of the late Sir Robert Peel . . . At twelve o'clock the Exhibitions were in full swing – gongs, rattles, drums, trumpets etc are vying with each other . . . The special trains are pouring forth their thousands after thousands as the ponderous vehicles reach the station . . . The Exhibition is also accompanied by that extraordinary race of men the Zulu Kaffirs, or Wild Men of Africa.

NOTTINGHAM MERCURY AND GENERAL ADVERTISER
2 OCTOBER 1850

The lads in their hundreds to
Ludlow come in for the fair,
There's men from the barn and the forge and the mill
and the fold,
The lads for the girls and the lads for the liquor are there,
And there with the rest are the lads that will never be old.

A. E. HOUSMAN (1859–1936)

JUNE

Punch and Judy shows

A PUNCH AND JUDY puppet show was part of any village fair and could always be found at seaside resorts. This famous pair along with their dog Toby were probably introduced into England from the Continent. The typical Punch and Judy show was performed on a miniature, portable stage, usually covered with striped canvas. Punch, with his hunchback and hooked nose, remained on the stage throughout the performance, doing battle with a series of characters including his wife Judy, baby, priest, doctor, policeman and hangman. Audiences delighted to see the feisty old Punch beat and whack his way through life with his stick, somehow always managing to triumph against all odds.

Have you a penny? well then, stay!
Haven't you any? don't go away!
Punch holds receptions all through the day,
Speaking aloud to gather a crowd,
Scolding at Toby, beating his wife,
Frightening the Constable out of his life,
And making jokes in a terrible passion,
As is Mr Punch's peculiar fashion;
For this is his old, delightful plan
Of getting as many pence as he can.

FELIX LEIGH (1883)

JUNE

22

23

24

25

26

27

28

28 JUNE 1837
*The coronation of
Queen Victoria*

NOTES

_____

❧
29

_____

❧
30

_____

❧
NOTES

_____

❧
_____

❧
_____

❧
_____

❧
_____

❧
_____

Now merry Punch
with voice so strong,
He is all for fun
and chaffing,
If you listen to his song
You'll burst your sides
with laughing.

ANONYMOUS

JULY

 WITH THE COMING of the railways, a trip to the seaside became an annual event for almost every Victorian family. Each summer Brighton, Blackpool, Margate and Scarborough and many other seaside towns would fill up with visitors from London and the larger cities.

_____ ☀ 1 _____

_____ ☀ 2 _____

_____ ☀ 3 _____

_____ ☀ 4 _____

_____ ☀ 5 _____

_____ ☀ 6 _____

_____ ☀ 7 _____

_____ ☀ _____
NOTES

_____ ☀ _____

The Seaside

PROPER BEHAVIOUR at the seaside was strictly enforced. Men and women were not allowed to mingle on the beach or even swim together. Any boat approaching the women's area of the beach could be fined. Bathing costumes were designed for modesty, not sport. Men were expected to keep their chests covered, and women were covered from head to toe with cumbersome flannel or serge bathing costumes. When soaked with water, these costumes became so heavy as to make swimming almost impossible; the Victorian lady had to be content with merely bobbing up and down in the water.

I took the train to Brighton
I walked beside the sea,
And thirty thousand Londoners
Were there along with me.

ANONYMOUS

Oh, I do like to be beside
the seaside,
Oh, I do like to be beside
the sea.
Oh, I do like to stroll along
the prom, prom, prom,
Where the brass bands play,
tiddley pom pom pom!

POPULAR SONG

JULY

The Coast

*A*lice had been to the seaside once in her life,
and had come to the general conclusion that,
wherever you go on the English coast you find a number of
bathing-machines in the sea, some children digging in the
sand with wooden spades, then a row of lodging-houses, and
behind them a railway station.

LEWIS CARROLL (1832–1898)
ALICE IN WONDERLAND

JULY

8

9

9 JULY 1845
Charles Darwin born

10

11

12

13

14

——————————— ✤ ———————————
15

——————————— ✤ ———————————
16

——————————— ✤ ———————————
17

17 JULY 1841

The first issue of
Punch *goes on sale*

——————————— ✤ ———————————
18

——————————— ✤ ———————————
19

——————————— ✤ ———————————
20

——————————— ✤ ———————————
21

BATHING MACHINES were a uniquely Victorian invention. These wooden changing cabins on wheels were drawn to the water's edge by horses. On the seaward side was a type of hood that projected out over the water, screening a woman bather as she slipped into the sea. These cumbersome contraptions became more and more unpopular with time and were regularly the subject of attack by *Punch* magazine:

> *It is not aesthetic, not yet picturesque.*
> *'Tis heavy, and cumbrous, expensive, grotesque,*
> *And I feel very certain that never was seen,*
> *Such an old-fashioned thing as a Bathing Machine . . .*
> *Oh, a hideous hutch is the Bathing Machine.*

PUNCH (1883)

JULY

_____ 22 _____

_____ 23 _____

_____ 24 _____

_____ 25 _____

_____ 26 _____

_____ 27 _____

_____ 28 _____

_____

NOTES

Keepsakes

THE VICTORIANS collected shells, seaweed and other objects from the sea as souvenirs of their visit to the seaside. Back home, women decorated picture frames, boxes and needle cases with shells and designed seaweed pictures. A common theme was a basket of seaweed, usually inscribed with this little verse:

Oh, call us not weeds, but flowers of the sea,
For lovely and gay and bright-tinted are we,
Our blush is as deep as the rose by thy bowers,
Then call us not weeds – we are ocean's gay flowers.

See what a lovely shell,
Small and pure as a pearl,
Lying close to my foot,
Frail, but a work divine,
Made so fairly well
With delicate spire and whorl,
How exquisitely minute,
A miracle of design!

ALFRED, LORD TENNYSON
(1809–1892)
THE SHELL

Besides these natural keepsakes, there were plenty of items for sale to remind a visitor of the seaside holiday. Spun glass ornaments, shell animals, china plates inscribed with someone's name or with a 'A Present from Brighton' made ideal gifts for the folks back home. The seaside souvenir merchants did a brisk trade. Some Victorians, like Jerome K. Jerome, were astute enough to foresee that for future generations these souvenirs would become valued treasures.

The blue-and-white mugs of the present-day roadside inn will be hunted up, all cracked and chipped, and sold for their weight in gold, and rich people from Japan will buy up the 'Present from Ramsgate' and 'Souvenir from Margate', that may have escaped destruction, and take them back to Jedo as ancient English curios.

JEROME K. JEROME (1859–1927)
THREE MEN IN A BOAT

Notwithstanding all these delights of a seaside holiday, there were some who were decidedly unimpressed with life by the sea.

There are certain things – a spider, a ghost,
The income-tax, gout, an umbrella for three –
That I hate, but the thing I hate most
Is a thing they call the SEA.

LEWIS CARROLL (1832–1898)
A SEA DIRGE

JULY

_____ ❦ _____

29

_____ ❦ _____

30

_____ ❦ _____

31

_____ ❦ _____

NOTES

_____ ❦ _____

_____ ❦ _____

_____ ❦ _____

_____ ❦ _____

_____ ❦ _____

JULY

The Boarding House

A REGULAR FEATURE of any seaside holiday was the boarding-house. It became the butt of ridicule and jokes, portrayed as an uncomfortable, overcrowded and overpriced establishment run by a penny-pinching landlady. Nevertheless, the boarding-house was the temporary home for most Victorian holiday-makers during their stay at the seaside. Here they met up with fellow lodgers over meals or a game of cards and exchanged the news of the day and shared the local gossip.

I play a spade. – Such strange new faces
Are flocking in from near and far;
Such frights! – (Miss Dobbs holds all the aces) –
One can't imagine who they are:
The lodging at enormous prices, –
New donkeys, and another fly;
And Madame Bonbon out of ices,
Although we're scarcely in July:
We're quite as sociable as any,
But one old horse can scarcely crawl:
And really, where there are so many,
We can't tell where we ought to call.

W. M. PRAED (1802–1839)
ARRIVALS AT A WATERING-PLACE

Trips to the
Seaside were also
becoming popular in
America; however, the
Americans seemed to be somewhat
more relaxed in their approach to
bathing. There were no bathing machines,
and to the shock of visitors from Britain, men
and women swam together. Here is an intriguing
eye-witness account of the bathing customs at Long
Branch on the east coast of America:

*The shore, it seems, is too bold to admit bathing-
machines and the ladies have therefore recourse to
another mode of ensuring enjoyment of sea-bathing with
safety. The accommodation at Long Branch is almost
entirely at large boarding-houses, where all the company live
at a table d'hôte. It is customary for ladies on arriving to
look around among the married gentlemen, the first time they
meet at table, and to select the one her fancy leads her to
prefer as a protector in her proposed visit to the realms of
Neptune; she makes her request, which is always graciously
received, that he would lead her to taste the briny wave; but
another fair one must select the same protector, else the
arrangement cannot be complete as custom does not authorise
tête-à-tête immersions.*

FRANCES TROLLOPE (1780–1863)
DOMESTIC MANNERS IN AMERICA

JULY

AUGUST

HE LEISURED CLASS had long been able to afford the luxury of travel to the Continent with extended stays in their favourite countries. In almost every large European city, there were English communities where the social life was somewhat more relaxed than it was at home. The climate, scenery and history of other countries inspired many of the great poets of the era.

_____ ✦

1

_____ ✦

2

_____ ✦

3

_____ ✦

4

_____ ✦

5

_____ ✦

6

_____ ✦

7

_____ ✦

N O T E S

_____ ✦

So, after the sore torments of the route; –
Toothache, and headache, and the ache of the wind,
And huddled sleep, and smarting wakefulness,
And night, and day, and hunger sick at food,
And twenty-fold relays, and packages
To be unlocked, and passports to be found,
And heavy well-kept landscape; – we were glad
Because we entered Brussels in the sun.

DANTE GABRIEL ROSSETTI (1828–1882)
REACHING BRUSSELS

O love, what hours were thine and mine,
In lands of palm and southern pine;
   In lands of palm, of orange-blossom,
Of olive, aloe, and maize and vine.

*W*hat Roman strength Turbia show'd
In ruin, by the mountain road;
   How like a gem, beneath, the city
Of little Monaco, basking, glow'd.

ALFRED, LORD TENNYSON (1809–1892)
THE DAISY

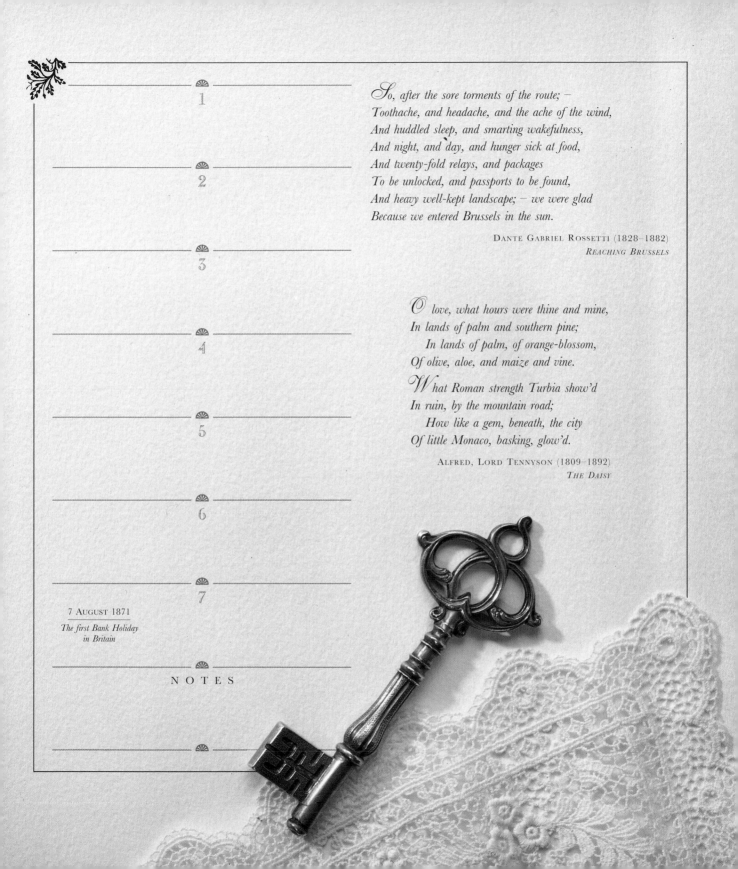

Travel

The image shows a postcard with the caption "Panorama sur la Seine pris vers la Tour Eiffel - A. P." / "of the Seine - Eiffel Tower in the distance"

AT THE BEGINNING of the Victorian era, travel to the Continent was in the privileged domain of the rich. But the railways and Thomas Cook changed all that. By the 1850s Thomas Cook's travel agency, with the help of special excursion rates offered by the rail companies, was able to offer relatively inexpensive conducted tours on the Continent. Cook agents guided the inexperienced and largely middle-class travellers through the tricky maze of foreign etiquette, currency and languages and showed them all the sights that ought to be seen, while explaining why they ought to be seen:

> *Follow the man from Cook's*
> *Ladies and gentlemen leave it to me,*
> *Follow the man from Cook's*
> *Nobody else is as clever as he,*
> *Follow the man from Cook's.*
> *And whether your stay be short or long,*
> *He'll show you the sights. He can't go wrong.*
> *It's twenty to one, you've plenty of fun,*
> *So follow the man from Cook's.*
>
> POPULAR SONG

AUGUST

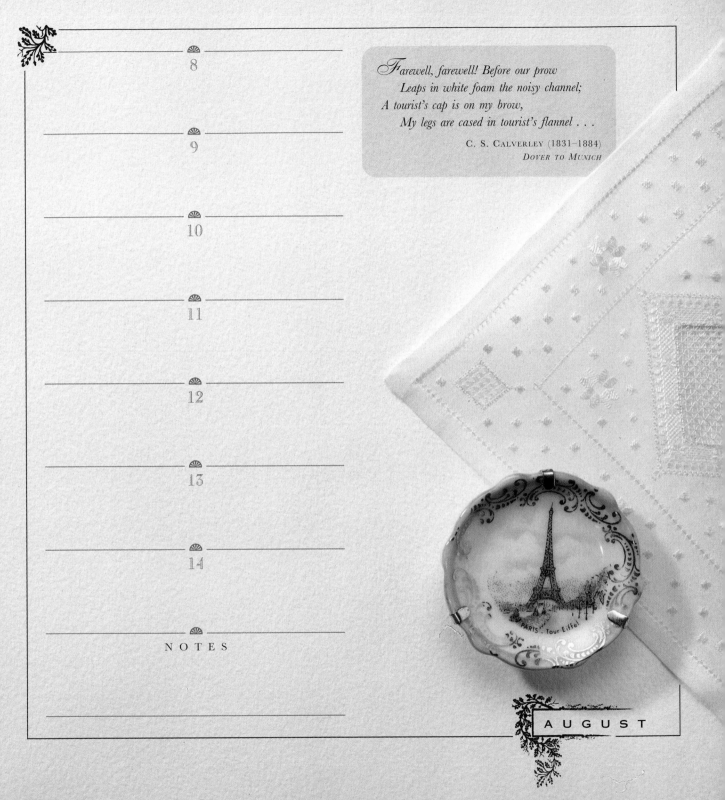

8

9

10

11

12

13

14

NOTES

Farewell, farewell! Before our prow
Leaps in white foam the noisy channel;
A tourist's cap is on my brow,
My legs are cased in tourist's flannel . . .

C. S. CALVERLEY (1831–1884)
DOVER TO MUNICH

AUGUST

America

HISTORICAL AND CULTURAL ties made America a desirable travel destination for many Victorians. They were fascinated by its vast landscapes and wild frontiers as well as the wonders of its technological inventiveness.

Gigantic daughter of the West
We drink to thee across the flood . . .
For art not thou of English blood?

ALFRED, LORD TENNYSON (1809–1892)
HANDS ALL ROUND

Republic of the West
Enlightened, free, sublime,
Unquestionably best
Production of our time.

The telephone is thine,
And thine the Pullman car,
The caucus, the divine
Intense electric star.

JAMES KENNETH STEPHEN
(1859–1892)
ENGLAND AND AMERICA

AUGUST

15

16

17

18

19

20

21

NOTES

22

23

24

25

26

27

28

NOTES

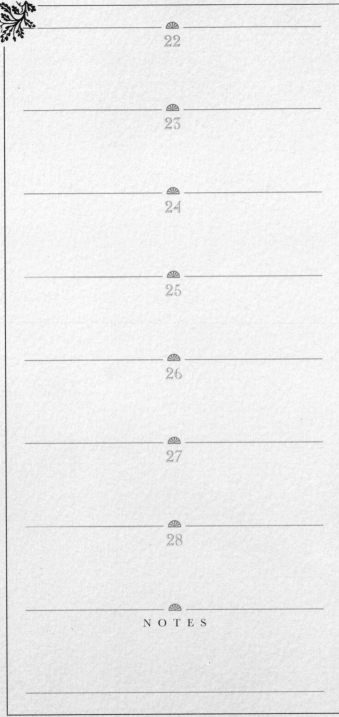

*English people
are far more
interested in
American
barbarism than
they are in American
civilization . . . They have been
known to prefer Buffaloes to Boston.*

OSCAR WILDE (1854–1900)
THE AMERICAN INVASION

AUGUST

_____
29

_____
30

_____
31

NOTES

_____

_____

_____

_____

_____

AUGUST

America

Though I have kind invitations enough to visit America, I could not, even for a couple of months, live in a country so miserable as to possess no castles.

JOHN RUSKIN (1819–1900)
PRAETERITA

Not all Victorians were as disparaging of America. For many the beauty and diversity of this vast untamed land stood in stark contrast to the small and ordered island from which they had travelled.

I am lost in wonder and amazement. It is not a country but a world . . . The West I liked best. The people are stronger, fresher, saner than the rest. They are ready to be taught. The surroundings of nature have instilled in them a love of the beautiful, which but needs development and direction. The East I found a feeble reflex of Europe, in fact, I may say that I was in America for a month before I saw an American.

OSCAR WILDE (1854–1900)
QUOTED IN *ST LOUIS DAILY GLOBE-DEMOCRAT.*
26 FEBRUARY 1882

In contrast, Americans who had travelled to Britain were left in wonder and amazement at the comparative lack of space:

Darn your little island! When I was there I found it so little I was afeerd I should tumble off. Look you, siree! We've steam-boats enough at St Louis to tow Great Britain out in to the Atlantic and stick her fast; – opposite New York Harbour.

AN ANONYMOUS CITIZEN OF ST LOUIS
QUOTED IN *LIFE AND LIBERTY IN AMERICA*
(1859) BY CHARLES MACKAY.

The great characteristic of English scenery . . . I should call density of feature. There is no waste of details; everything in the landscape is something particular – has a history, has played a part, has a value to the imagination.

HENRY JAMES (1843–1916)
ABBEYS AND CASTLES (1877)

The wildest things in England are more than half-tame.

NATHANIEL HAWTHORNE (1804–1864)
OUR OLD HOME

AUGUST

SEPTEMBER

URING THE VICTORIAN PERIOD, hundreds of thousands of people left Britain in search of a better life in the open spaces of colonial countries such as Canada, Australia and New Zealand. This was the time in which the Victorian Empire was built and spread across the globe. But in these strange and distant lands, thoughts must have many times turned homeward.

Empire

O England, country of my heart's desire,
  Land of the hedgerow and the village spire,
Land of thatched cottages and murmuring bees,
  And wayside inns where one may take one's ease,
Of village greens where cricket may be played,
  And fat old spaniels sleeping in the shade. —
O homeland, far away across the main,
  How would I love to see your face again! —
Your daisied meadows and your grassy hills,
  Your primrose banks, your parks, your tinkling rills,
Your copses where the purple bluebells grow,
  Your quiet lanes where lovers loiter so,
Your cottage-gardens with their wallflowers' scent,
  Your swallows 'neath the eaves, your sweet content!
And 'mid the fleecy clouds that o'er you spread,
  Listen, the skylark singing overhead . . .
That's the old country, that's the old home!
  You never forget it wherever you roam.

E. V. Lucas (1868–1938)
The Old Country

The earth is a place on which England is found,
And you find it however you twirl the globe round;
For the spots are all red and the rest is grey,
And that is the meaning of Empire Day.

G. K. Chesterton (1874–1936)
Song of Education

1

2

3

4

5

6

7

NOTES

SEPTEM

_____ ⚜ _____
8

_____ ⚜ _____
9

_____ ⚜ _____
10

_____ ⚜ _____
11

_____ ⚜ _____
12

12 SEPTEMBER 1846

The poet Elizabeth Barrett elopes with Robert Browning

_____ ⚜ _____
13

_____ ⚜ _____
14

_____ ⚜ _____
NOTES

SEPTEMBER

Empire

Till now the name of names, England, the name of might,
Flames from the austral fires to the bounds of the boreal nights,
And the call of her morning drum goes in a girdle of sound,
Like the voice of the sun in song, the great globe round and round.

WILLIAM ERNEST HENLEY (1849–1903)
RHYMES AND RHYTHMS

VICTORIAN BRITAIN ruled over the largest empire the world has ever seen. The British looked upon these overseas colonies with pride and with the sincere belief that through their administration of this vast empire they were bringing peace, good order and freedom to a large part of the world.

But as the days of empire wore on, doubts about Britain's role as a colonial master began to creep in.

The gangrene of colonial rowdyism is infecting us, and the habit of repressing liberty in weak nations is endangering our own. I should be glad to see the end.

WILFRED SCAWEN BLUNT (1840–1922)
DIARY, 9 JANUARY 1896

_____ ⊛ 15

_____ ⊛ 16

_____ ⊛ 17

17 September 1848

First train service linking London and Birmingham

_____ ⊛ 18

_____ ⊛ 19

_____ ⊛ 20

_____ ⊛ 21

⊛

NOTES

_____

_____

The Mother of Colonies has a wonderful gift for alienating the affections of her own household by neglect.

RUDYARD KIPLING (1865–1936)
FROM *TIDEWAY TO TIDEWAY*

SEPTEMBER

India and the Raj

IN 1857, the Crown took over the administration of India from the East India Company and ruled this, its most prosperous colony, through a series of viceroys. This was the beginning of the British 'Raj'. Queen Victoria was proclaimed 'Empress of India', and India became her most precious 'jewel in the crown'.

George wonders every day how we are allowed to keep this country a week.

EMILY EDEN,
WIFE OF GEORGE EDEN,
GOVERNOR OF INDIA
(1835–1841)
LETTER
21 JUNE 1841

It is only when you get to see and realise what India really is, – that she is the strength and greatness of England – it is only then that you feel that every nerve a man may strain, every energy he may put forward, cannot be devoted to a nobler purpose than keeping the tight cords that hold India to ourselves.

LORD CURZON (1859–1925)
VICEROY OF INDIA FROM 1899 TO 1905

Our title to India depends on a first condition, that our being there is profitable to the Indian nations; and on a second condition, that we can make them see and understand that it is profitable.

W. E. GLADSTONE (1809–1898)

SEPTEMBER

_____ ☙ _____
22

_____ ☙ _____
23

_____ ☙ _____
24

_____ ☙ _____
25

_____ ☙ _____
26

_____ ☙ _____
27

_____ ☙ _____
28

_____ ☙ _____

NOTES

_____

Most Victorians accepted the British rule over India as their right by virtue of their superiority. Rudyard Kipling, who spent much of his life in India and saw first-hand the British Raj in operation, was convinced of the moral duty of the 'White Man' to govern conquered nations.

Take up the White Man's burden –
Send forth the best ye breed –
Go bind your sons to exile
To serve your captives' need;
To wait in heavy harness
On fluttered folk and wild –
Your new-caught, sullen peoples,
Half devil and half child.

Take up the White Man's burden –
Ye dare not stoop to less –
Nor call too loud on Freedom
To cloak your weariness;
By all ye cry or whisper,
By all ye leave or do,
The silent, sullen peoples
Shall weigh your Gods
_   and you._

RUDYARD KIPLING
(1865–1936)
THE WHITE MAN'S
BURDEN

Missionaries and Explorers

DURING THE VICTORIAN era it was generally accepted that other nations, particularly India and Africa, would benefit from Britain's superior technology as well as its culture and religion. Explorers set out to map uncharted territories and open them up to British trade and influence. Exploration and missionary zeal were closely entwined, for Christianity was seen as another of the many benefits that Britain could bestow on the natives of these newly discovered lands. The greatest Victorian explorer and missionary was David Livingstone. He made very few converts, but he was held as a national hero for his achievements in mapping previously unknown parts of the African continent. Livingstone became the first European to cross Africa from east to west and back again.

29

30

NOTES

SEPTEMBER

From Greenland's icy mountains;
From India's coral strand,
Where Afric's sunny fountains
Roll down their golden sand;
From many an ancient river,
From many a palmy plain,
They call us to deliver
Their land from error's chain.

REGINALD HEBER (1783–1826)
ENGLISH BISHOP OF CALCUTTA
MISSIONARY HYMN

TRAVELLING SECOND CLASS – THE PARTING
ABRAHAM SOLOMON (1824–1862)

If I were a Cassowary
On the plains of Timbuctoo,
I would eat a missionary,
Coats and bands and hymn-book too.

BISHOP SAMUEL WILBERFORCE
(1805–1873)
EPIGRAM

SEPTEMBER

He wrote for certain papers
which, as everybody knows,
Is worse than slaving in a shop
or scaring off the crows.

RUDYARD KIPLING (1865–1936)
DELILAH

OCTOBER

DURING VICTORIAN TIMES, newspapers were becoming cheaper and easier to produce because of technological innovations. Many new daily papers appeared and millions of new newspaper readers were created thanks to an increase in leisure time and a higher standard of education.

Newspapers

1

2

3 OCTOBER 1896

*Queen Victoria and the
Tsar's family filmed in
the first royal 'moving
cinematograph
photographs'*

3

4

5

6

7

NOTES

THIS LITTLE VERSE is typical of the general praise Victorians had for journalism and newspapers:

> *The Press - the Press - the glorious Press,*
> *It makes the nations free?*
> *Before it tyrants prostrate fall*
> *And proud oppressors flee!*
> *In what a state of wretchedness*
> *Without it should we be;*
> *And can we then too highly prize*
> *The source of liberty?*
>
> ANONYMOUS

However, not everyone shared these sentiments. Charles Dickens, in spite of the fact that many of his novels first appeared in serialized form in newspapers, had this to say about them:

> *They are so filthy and bestial that no honest man would admit one into his house for a water-closet doormat.*
>
> CHARLES DICKENS
> (1812–1870)

OCTOBER

Family Entertainment

THE VICTORIAN FAMILY enjoyed quiet amusements such as cards and board games at the end of the day. Often one member would read aloud as the rest of the family seated themselves round the fire. Or everyone would gather at the piano and sing.

One of the best-loved parlour songs was *Home, Sweet Home*, which was written for the opera *Clari; or the Maid of Milan*. The music was composed by Sir Henry Bishop and the lyrics by John Howard Payne, an American actor. *Home, Sweet Home* sold over ten thousand copies within the year of its first public performance. Unfortunately for Payne, he had sold his libretto for the opera for an outright fee, so he received no royalties for his famous song.

'Mid pleasures and palaces though we may roam,
Be it ever so humble, there's no place like home;
A charm from the sky seems to hallow us there,
Which, seek through the world, is ne'er met with elsewhere.
  Home, Home, sweet, sweet Home!
There's no place like Home! there's no place like Home!

An exile from home, splendour dazzles in vain;
O, give me my lowly thatched cottage again!
The birds singing gayly, that came to my call —
Give me them, — and the peace of mind, dearer that all!
  Home, Home, sweet, sweet Home!
There's no place like Home! there's no place like Home!

JOHN HOWARD PAYNE (1791–1852)
HOME, SWEET HOME

Come read to me some poem, Some simple and heartfelt lay,
That shall soothe this restless feeling, And banish the thoughts of day.

HENRY WADSWORTH LONGFELLOW (1807–1882)
THE DAY IS DONE

OCTOBER

_____

_____

8

_____

9

9 October 1899

The first motor bus in London

_____

10

_____

11

_____

12

_____

13

_____

14

_____

NOTES

When you are old and grey and full of sleep, And nodding by the fire, take down this book, And slowly read, and dream of the soft look Your eyes had once, and of their shadows deep . . .

W.B. YEATS (1865–1939)
WHEN YOU ARE OLD

OCTOBER

Family Entertainment

OTHER FAVOURITE parlour songs were Thomas Moore's *Oft in the Stilly Night* and Tennyson's *Come into the Garden, Maud*, set to music by Michael Balfe.

Come into the garden, Maud,
For the black bat, night, has flown,
Come into the garden, Maud,
I am here at the gate alone;
And the woodbine spices are wafted abroad,
And the musk of the rose is blown.

For a breeze of morning moves,
And the planet of Love is on high,
Beginning to faint in the light that she loves
On a bed of daffodil sky,
To faint in the light of the sun she loves,
To faint in his light, and to die . . .

ALFRED, LORD TENNYSON (1809–1892)
COME INTO THE GARDEN, MAUD

15

15 OCTOBER 1895
Britain's first motor car show held at Tunbridge Wells, Kent

16

16 OCTOBER 1854
Oscar Wilde born

17

18

19

20

21

NOTES

22

23

24

25

26

27

28

NOTES

*Oft in the stilly night
Ere slumber's chain has bound me,
Fond Memory brings the light
Of other days around me:
    The smiles, the tears
    Of Boyhood's years,
The words of love then spoken;
    The eyes that shone,
    Now dimm'd and gone,
The cheerful hearts now broken!
Oft in the stilly night
Ere slumber's chain has bound me,
Fond Memory brings the light
Of other days around me.*

THOMAS MOORE (1779–1852)
THE LIGHT OF OTHER DAYS

OCTOBER

Theatre

DURING THE VICTORIAN PERIOD, acting and the theatre were gaining a degree of respectability and professionalism. New theatres were opening up, with their sumptuous decor, plush red seats and the soft glow of gas lighting. Here audiences could see magnificent performances by the great actors of the day such as Henry Irving and Ellen Terry. Henry Irving, in partnership with Ellen Terry, produced and appeared in plays at the Lyceum for more than thirty years.

The Victorians preferred drama that was melodramatic and sentimental in style. They also liked lavish and costly productions. One production, *The Fall of Khartoum and Death of General Gordon*, had one hundred camels, two hundred horses and two military bands all appearing nightly. Not surprisingly, it lost money.

The comic operas by William Gilbert and Arthur Sullivan were Victorian favourites that are still enjoyed today. In 1881, Gilbert and Sullivan's Savoy Theatre became the first building to be lit entirely by electric lights.

OCTOBER

29

30

31

NOTES

AT THE THEATRE
James Hayllar (1829–1920)

Acting is therefore the lowest form of the arts, if it is an art at all.
GEORGE MOORE (1852–1933)

Behind the curtain's mystic fold the golden future lies unrolled.
BRET HARTE (1836–1902)
ADDRESS AT THE OPENING OF CALIFORNIA THEATRE,
SAN FRANCISCO 19 JANUARY 1870

OCTOBER

NOVEMBER

USIC HALLS were largely working-class places of entertainment with a fun-loving, irreverent atmosphere. There were singers, dancers, conjurers, acrobats and comedians who pattered with the audiences. Music halls specialized in the comic song of about a dozen verses that told a story or commented on some current political event. There was usually a catchy chorus at the end of each verse so that the audience could join in.

NOVEMBER

Music Halls

1

2

3

4

5

6

7

N ORDER to curb any excesses, some music halls set certain guidelines for their performers. The house rules for one establishment warned the artists that no offensive allusions were to be made to any member of the Royal Family, Members of Parliament, or German Princes, among others. But despite these standards of behaviour, things could still sometimes get quite lively.

The music hall was a rough and ready place. Sometimes the interchange between performer and audience could get quite fierce. I remember one evening when the singer stopped mid-song to deliver a colourful tirade to a section of the audience whose rowdy behaviour had interrupted her performance. Her vitriolic reprimand won her respectful silence for the rest of the evening.

ROGER CONNOLLY (1848–1922)
UNPUBLISHED MEMOIRS

NOTES

NOVEMBER

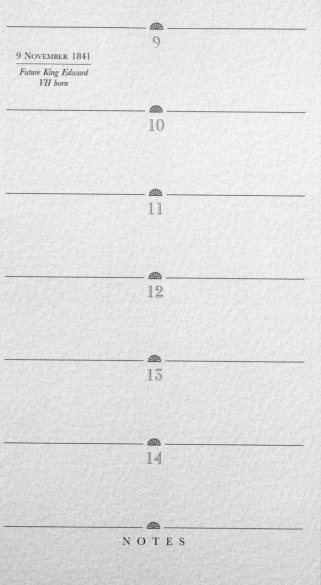

8

9

9 NOVEMBER 1841

Future King Edward VII born

10

11

12

Wild West Shows

13

Near the very end of the Victorian era William Cody, generally known as Buffalo Bill, brought his Wild West show to Britain, where it was a huge success. There was even a private Royal Command performance for the Queen. The show with its cast of cowboys, Indians and sharp-shooters re-enacted famous historic events of the American west such as Custer's Last Stand.

14

NOTES

NOVEMBER

I was about twelve years old when my father took me to see Buffalo Bill and his Wild West Show in London. It was the most exciting thing that had happened in my short life. I knew all about Buffalo Bill and his exploits in the American West. It was said that when he was hunting buffalo to provide meat for the men who were building the railway across the West, he once killed sixty-nine animals in a single day. That's how he got the name Buffalo Bill. His reputation was legendary. When he was acting as scout for the cavalry, he fought a hand-to-hand duel with the son of a Cheyenne chief and killed him. These were the kind of stories that sparked the imagination of a young boy living in a crowded city, where the adventure of the American wilderness seemed like a dream.

The highlight of the show was when the Indians galloped into the arena, their faces covered in war paint, their tomahawks held on high, riding their horses bareback. After much whooping and hollering and menacing gestures on the part of the Indians, in rode the Buffalo Bill on his white horse leading his band of cavalry troops. There followed the inevitable shoot-out and the equally inevitable Indian defeat and surrender. But it was the stuff of magic and my head was filled with visions of the Wild West for a long time after.

GEORGE NELSON (1877–1949)
UNPUBLISHED REMINISCENCES

NOVEMBER

15

16

17

18

19

20

21

Very tiring to the eyes, but worth a headache to have such a marvel.

QUEEN VICTORIA, AFTER WATCHING A FILM OF HER
DIAMOND JUBILEE PROCESSION (1897)

NOVEMBER

Photography and Cinema

PHOTOGRAPHY AND CINEMA were the technological marvels of the late Victorian age. The grim faces and stiff postures seen in early photographs were the result of being clamped into position to prevent movement during the long exposures. But things advanced quickly; photographic techniques improved and the next major advance was the moving pictures, or biographs, as they were called. In 1896 the Lumière brothers of France showed three short films at the Empire Theatre in London. Soon music halls were showing short films of news and other events at the end of their regular programmes.

It is astonishing how soon one grows accustomed to new wonders. Otherwise the exhibition of animated photographs now on view at the West Street concert hall would be nothing short of sensational. As it is, we have been trained in a brief space of time to accept photographic records of events, showing all the life and movement and excitement of a scene, almost as a matter of course as a newspaper record. The Biograph has speedily taken a place in our life as a supplemental chronicler of the more notable events of the day in all quarters of the world, and a highly interesting chronicler it is, enabling us to realize the spirit of scenes with an actuality and vividness hitherto unattainable.

BRIGHTON HERALD, (DECEMBER 1900)

NOVEMBER

Ice Skating

DURING THE LATE Victorian times there was an ice skating boom, or 'rinkomania', as it was called. Skating was particularly attractive to young couples because it gave them a chance to skate arm-in-arm out into the rink and away from the watchful eyes of their chaperons. But not everyone was so adept at the sport:

Mr Winkle, with his face and hands blue with the cold, had been forcing a gimlet into the soles of his feet, and putting his skates on, with the points behind, and getting the straps into a very complicated and entangled state, with the assistance of Mr Snodgrass, who knew rather less about skates than a Hindoo. At length, however, with the assistance of Mr Weller, the unfortunate skates were firmly screwed and buckled on, and Mr Winkle was raised to his feet.

WINTER FUN
FRANK DADD
(1851–1929)

22

23

24

25

26

27

28

NOTES

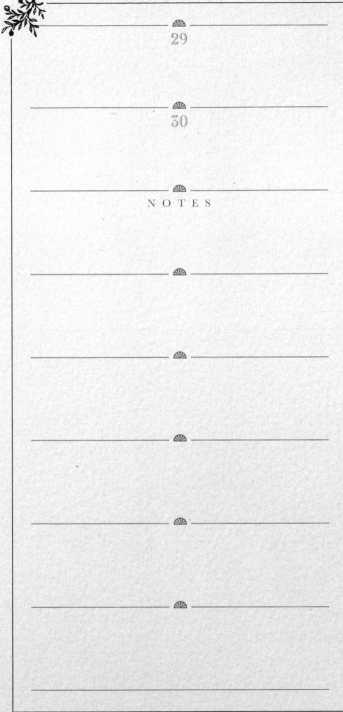

_____

✾
29

_____

✾
30

_____

✾
NOTES

_____

✾

_____

✾

_____

✾

_____

✾

_____

✾

_____

'Now, then, Sir,' said Sam, in an encouraging tone; 'off vith you, and show 'em how to do it.'

'Stop, Sam, stop!' said Mr Winkle, trembling violently, and clutching hold of Sam's arms with a grasp of a drowning man. 'How slippery it is, Sam!'

'Not an uncommon thing upon ice, Sir,' replied Mr Weller. 'Hold up, sir!'

This last observation of Mr Weller's bore reference to a demonstration Mr Winkle made at that instant, of a frantic desire to throw his feet in the air, and dash the back of his head on the ice.

'These — these — are very awkward skates; ain't they, Sam?' inquired Mr Winkle staggering.

'I'm afeerd ther's a orkard gen'l'm'n in 'em, Sir,' replied Sam.

CHARLES DICKENS (1812–1870)
PICKWICK PAPERS

NOVEMBER

DECEMBER

ANY OF THE CHRISTMAS TRADITIONS we enjoy today began with the Victorians. The Royal Family set the example in Christmas festivities, and households throughout the country tried to imitate them in every way.

1

2

3

4

5

6

7

NOTES

Christmas Cards and Presents

I *t has created quite a new trade, and has opened up a new field of labour for artists, lithographers, engravers, printers, ink and pasteboard makers . . . All the year round brains are at work devising new designs and inventing novelties.*

THE TIMES (1883)

This 'new trade' was the Christmas card. In 1843 the first Christmas cards appeared in a London art shop, designed and produced by the shop's owner, Henry Cole. These first cards were rather expensive, and since there was no established custom for sending Christmas greetings, they remained largely unsold. But gradually the idea took hold, thanks to cheaper card production and the half-penny postal rate.

'Twas the night before Christmas, when all through the house
Not a creature was stirring not even a mouse;
The stockings were hung by the chimney with care
In hope that St Nicholas soon would be there.

PROFESSOR CLEMENT C. MOORE (1779–1863)
A VISIT FROM ST NICHOLAS

DECEMBER

The Christmas Tree

THE CHRISTMAS TREE was introduced from Germany by Prince Albert. When in 1848, an engraving published by *The London Illustrated News* showed Queen Victoria and Prince Albert with their children gathered around a Christmas tree, the fashion for them quickly spread. Presents, sweets and other trifles were tied to the branches; on Christmas Day the tree candles were lit. During the 1890s the introduction of electric 'fairy' lights on the tree greatly reduced the number of Christmas fire accidents.

I have been looking on this evening at a merry company of children assembled around that pretty German toy, A Christmas Tree. The tree was planted in the middle of a great round table, and towered high above our heads. It was brilliantly lighted by a multitude of little tapers; and everywhere sparkled and glittered with bright objects. There were rosy cheeked dolls, hiding behind the green leaves; and there were real watches . . . dangling from innumerable twigs . . . in short, as a pretty child, before me, delightedly whispered to another pretty child, her bosom friend, 'There was everything, and more.'

CHARLES DICKENS (1812–1870)
HOUSEHOLD WORDS

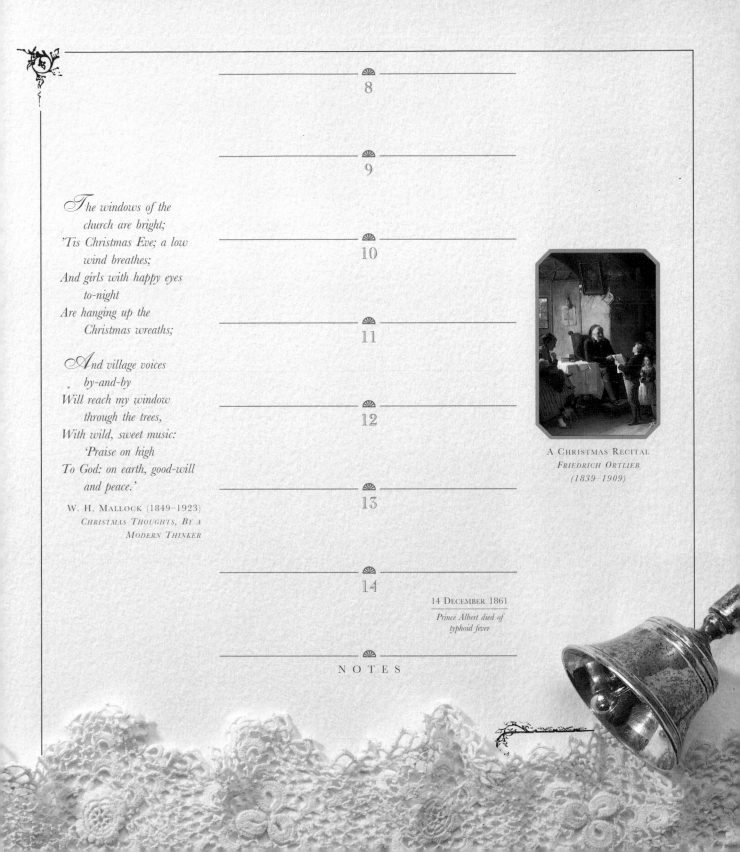

———— ❀ ————
8

———— ❀ ————
9

———— ❀ ————
10

———— ❀ ————
11

———— ❀ ————
12

———— ❀ ————
13

———— ❀ ————
14

———— ❀ ————
N O T E S

*The windows of the
church are bright;
'Tis Christmas Eve; a low
wind breathes;
And girls with happy eyes
to-night
Are hanging up the
Christmas wreaths;*

*And village voices
by-and-by
Will reach my window
through the trees,
With wild, sweet music:
'Praise on high
To God: on earth, good-will
and peace.'*

W. H. MALLOCK (1849–1923)
*CHRISTMAS THOUGHTS, BY A
MODERN THINKER*

A CHRISTMAS RECITAL
FRIEDRICH ORTLIEB
(1839–1909)

14 DECEMBER 1861
*Prince Albert died of
typhoid fever*

Santa Claus

ONE OF THE MOST POPULAR Christmas card images was Father Christmas, or Santa Claus. With the myth of Santa Claus came the idea of exchanging gifts at Christmas. By the 1890s Santa was appearing in person, with his red coat and long white beard, distributing gifts to delighted children.

He comes in the night! He comes
in the night!
He softly, silently comes;
While the little brown heads on the
pillows so white
Are dreaming of bugles and drums.
He cuts through the snow like a ship
through the foam,
While the white flakes around
him whirl;
Who tells him I know not, but he
findeth the home
Of each good little boy and girl.

His sleigh it is long, and deep, and wide;
It will carry a host of things
While dozens of drums hang over the side,
With the sticks sticking under the strings.
And yet not the sound of a drum is heard,
Not a bugle blast is blown,
As he mounts to the chimney-top like a bird,
And drops to the hearth like a stone.

ANONYMOUS

15

16

17

18

18 DECEMBER 1878

Joseph Swan
demonstrates his
incandescent
electric lamp

19

20

21

NOTES

DECEMBER

Christmas Dinner

Little Jack Horner
Sat in a corner,
Eating a Christmas pie,
He put in his thumb, and pulled out a plum,
And said 'What a good boy am I.'

NURSERY RHYME

PLUM PUDDING and mince pies – no Christmas seems complete without them – were all introduced into the Christmas menu by the Victorians. When turkey replaced roast swan on the Royal Christmas menu in the 1850s, it too became part of the Christmas ritual.

Plum pudding, or as the Victorians called it 'a pudding without plums' because the plums had long ago been replaced by raisins and currants, was made with the help of the whole family. Everyone took a turn stirring the pudding from east to west in honour of the Three Kings. Coins were hidden inside the pudding to add suspense to the Christmas meal. It was brought to the table ablaze and garnished with sprigs of holly.

God bless the master of this house,
Likewise the mistress too:
And all the little children
That round the table go.
Love and joy come to you,
And to your wassail too,
And God bless you and send you
A happy New Year.

CHRISTMAS CAROL

DECEMBER

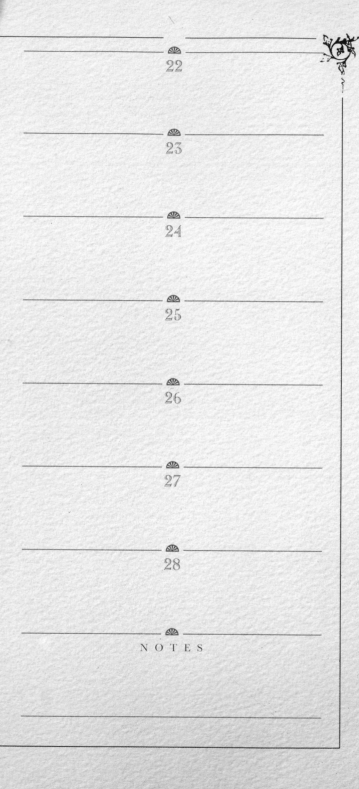

_____
_____ ✦
22

_____ ✦
23

_____ ✦
24

_____ ✦
25

_____ ✦
26

_____ ✦
27

_____ ✦
28

_____ ✦

NOTES

_____

Parties *and* Pantomime

THE CHRISTMAS PANTOMIME came into its
own during the Victorian age. It started on
Boxing Day at all major theatres throughout the
country, providing entertainment for the whole
family. The Christmas pantomime featured lavish
scenery, songs, dances, jokes and the closing comic
turn by the harlequin.

During the Christmas break from school,
children enjoyed parties that included games,
dancing, charades and perhaps a Punch and Judy
show. For adults there were plenty of balls and
dances to enjoy.

DECEMBER

29

30

30 December 1865
*Rudyard Kipling born
in Bombay, India*

31

☙

N O T E S

☙

☙

☙

☙

☙

Then old Fezziwig stood out to dance with
Mrs Fezziwig. Top couple, too, with a good stiff
piece of work cut out for them; three or four and twenty
pairs of partners; people who were not to be trifled with;
people who could dance and had no notion of walking.

But if it had been thrice as many – Oh, four times as
many – old Fezziwig would have been a match for them, so
would Mrs. Fezziwig. As to her, she was worthy to be his
partner in every sense of the term. If that's not high praise,
tell me higher and I'll use it. A positive light appeared to
issue from Fezziwig's calves. They shone in every part of the
dance like moons. You couldn't predict at any given time
what would become of them next . . .

When the clock struck eleven the domestic ball broke up.
Mr and Mrs. Fezziwig took their stations, one on either side
of the door, and shaking hands with every person
individually, as he or she went out, wished him or her
MERRY CHRISTMAS!

CHARLES DICKENS (1812–1870)
A CHRISTMAS CAROL

At Christmas play
and make good cheer,
For Christmas comes but
once a year.

D E C E M B E R

ACKNOWLEDGEMENTS
Special thanks are given to the following, for
their kind and generous help in supplying
photographic props.

THE BOOTH MUSEUM OF NATURAL HISTORY *31;*
STEPHANIE CARR-GOMM *101;* LORRAINE HARRISON *12;*
ADAM HOPKINS *93;* ROSE HOPKINS *13, 14, 16, 20, 25, 32, 36, 49,
51, 52, 72, 88, 99, 100;* PETER HOPKINS *17, 19, 21, 25, 27, 33,
37, 38, 43, 48, 55, 68, 73, 77, 81, 82, 83, 84, 85, 89, 94, 98;*
ANTHONY LANAWAY *92;* BOB LANAWAY *38, 39, 40, 41;*
LYANA LANAWAY *67, 86, 87, 104;* ROSEMARY LANAWAY *54, 56,
57, 58, 59, 60, 61, 62, 63, 65, 69, 105;* RAY MORRIS *95;*
MARGARET MOSS *10, 21, 35, 94, 103;* THE MULBERRY BUSH *11,
53;* KAREN RYECART *34, 35, 42, 72.* *Lace:* CHRISTINE MARR *10,
15, 16, 17, 18, 27, 28, 30, 31, 32, 39, 40, 41, 42, 44, 47, 49, 50,
53, 55, 58, 60, 62, 65, 67, 71, 73, 74, 77, 79, 80, 82, 88, 90, 92,
95, 96, 98, 101, 103;* POMPI PARRY *21, 24, 25, 35, 37, 57, 69.*
Picture credits: FINE ART PICTURE LIBRARY *10, 18, 26, 34, 50, 58,
66, 74, 81, 82, 89, 90, 93, 96, 98, 101;* E.T. ARCHIVES *42, 46.*

Designed, written and edited by

THE BRIDGEWATER BOOK COMPANY LTD.

Compiled and written by Joanne Jessop

Edited by Rhoda Nottridge

Designed by Peter Bridgewater

Photography by Guy Ryecart

Illustration by Lorraine Harrison

Page make-up by Chris Lanaway

Prop research and styling by Jane Lanaway

CLB Ref. 4307

Colour separations by Sussex Repro Ltd England

Printed and Bound in Spain by Graficas Estella

ISBN 1-85833-249-4